The Production of Haunted Space:

It's Meaning and Excavation

John G. Sabol
C.A.S.P.E.R. Research Center

Also by John Sabol

Ghost Excavator (2007)

Ghost Culture (2007)

Gettysburg Unearthed (2007)

Battlefield Hauntscape (2008)

The Anthracite Coal Region (2008)

The Politics of Presence (2008)

Bodies of Substance, Fragments of Memory (2009)

Phantom Gettysburg (2009)

Digging Deep (2009)

The Re-Haunting(s) of Gettysburg (2010)

The Haunted Theatre (2011)

Ghost Culture Too (2012)

Beyond the Paranormal (2012)

Digging-Up Ghosts (2nd publishing, 2013)

Burnside Bridge (2013)

The Gettysburg Experience (2013)

The Absence Above, A Presence Below (2013)

The Production of Haunted Space:

It's Meaning and Excavation

Ghost Excavator Books, Inc ™ ©

Bedford, Pennsylvania, USA

ISBN-13: 978-1491203996
ISBN-10: 1491203994

Ghost Excavation Books, Inc. ™©
A division of C.A.S.P.E.R. Research Center™©,
Bedford, PA, USA
www.ghostexcavation.com

Preface

- Imagine social relations as acts of giving and receiving "signs".
- Imagine this sociality through time is merely the gap between event and its subsequent manifestation through a recognition of "signs".
- Imagine this potential sociality through time is a haunting.
- Imagine the process of "reading" the meaning of such "signs" involves the understanding of what "signs" do, and how they come into play in the production of particular spaces.

The analysis of haunted space begins with a history of what happened there. It is the placing of people and their culture in the production of that space. It is what remains, perhaps years, decades, or even centuries after the events of that production of space has ended.

A Presence Waits in Space(s)

I have traveled far in exploring the past, yet have not ventured far from nearby spaces. This is not a question of distance and miles, but of depth. These journeys to the past have all been "excavations", most without breaking ground. Though travel there is often uneasy, getting there is often quick. Restrictions and access are not burdensome with official paperwork. Oft times, the trek leads to unexpected spaces and rewarding encounters. As William Chapman states:

> **"The past is at its best when it takes us to places that counsel and instruct, that show us who we are….that remind us of our connections to 'what happened here'".**

As an archaeologist, I deal with these past journeys by working with what remains. This work is mostly piecemeal, traces and fragments encountered for the most part during the journey. This doesn't make the interaction any less rewarding or sociable. As I (we) walk these spaces, we produce them anew, tied to what remains. The encounter may be brief, a physical presence (such as a discarded object), or a sensory presence (perhaps a certain sound or smell).

Large or small, brief or prolonged, they inscribe a passage of time as a space presents itself, and we produce a space. At that precise moment, a border has been crossed, and a "sign" of communication has begun. And this "crossing" is not always (or mostly) physical. As Sir Simon Marsden has said (and has revealed in countless spectacular images):

> **"In the remote, quieter corners of our landscape there is a strange feeling that we are not alone, as we pass by some ruined mansion or moonlit abbey at nightfall, we know that within the crumbling walls there still lurk dark spirits from the distant past....watching....waiting" (1994:10).**

Photo 1: What (or "Who") is Waiting in These Ruins?

<u>Photo 2</u>: Or in These?

Knowing some history of a particular space, remembering an event there, or recalling a story (perhaps from folklore) transforms that space, and unfolds time. The act of recall enfolds us into the palimpsest of the space. What we do next determines its future destiny as a new production of the space. We begin to haunt that space with our presence there, and the fieldwork that we do there.

Building and sharing these encounters is a means to revive past presence. It is also a revision of what remains, and how this may be different from what others have envisioned there. The production process is a creative event, not a "paranormal" one. But it is filled with cautionary tales. We must make certain what we intend to convey to others (both <u>before</u> and <u>after</u> us) as a "sign" of what remains during our brief encounter there.

The production in (of) space is a means of revising (revitalizing) it, a way of exploring the possibilities of how a space might be different from what others have reported and experienced (or even imagined). In this way, historical knowledge, cultural expression, and presence, and what remains of the past is recast. It is a new page in a palimpsest of occupation. This is a sign of a <u>normal</u> flow of information, a reality check of "what happened there".

This is a way of doing human history (apart from the historian's trade), and understanding human culture and behavior. It is also a way of remembering through the construction of social traditions and, in the production process, the labeling of personal and social identities within that space. In this sense, we produce the space that we explore. In this book, the production of words will perform the same function: the production, exploration, and analysis of spaces as being "haunted".

"Haunted space" is a generic "place name" that marks out a space as a symbolic site. These spaces, both occupied and abandoned, associate places with different types of symbols ("orb", shadows, acousmatic sounds, EVP). These symbols are used evocatively to tell stories (albeit ghost stories), and make commentary about past events and acts.

Central concerns to these stories are the following:

- Is there "truth" in the storytelling?
- Do we have all (or enough) "facts" about what is occurring there in a space that is perceived as a haunted space?

A fact is something done or made. It is a way of acting or doing. The "truth" resides in human activities, cultural expressions, and in the acts that make us human. Is an "orb", a "shadow", a sound a "sign" of a haunting? Does its manifestation express a (past) human activity?

Is knowledge about the past learned through these stories or through "signs" of presence that manifest in particular spaces after specific present acts? What is the relationship between these "signs" of a haunting, and how this haunted space is produced, apart from myth and folklore? How do we investigate such a place, and learn what remains of these past signs of cultural habitation? We must do more than simply record the "signs".

Answers must produce "facts", and a baseline toward the "truth". Answers must provide formulas for a paradigm for "truth". And it is this light that we can ascertain a context for interpretation.......

A "haunting" will be conceived here as a "sign" system. Actions, as manifestations of these "signs", involves the creation of social meaning, as this "sign system" forms the production of past space. What survives today, as part of this past production, is haunted space.

These "signs" that manifest are channels of communication from the past to the present. But its past (not contemporary) production must be clearly documented. Understanding and recording these haunting "signs" is an act of translating this communication. This translation must provide meaning in relation to past context.

The time is now for fieldwork to address these more serious matters of research (such as past context), that go beyond group entertainment and popular images of "hunting" the "ghost" with stereotyped displays of pseudoscience. It's time to develop a new trope for ghost research, one that incorporates the concept of production, theory, method, execution, material presence, and heritage to a field in dire need of guidance, orientation, and discipline.

It's time to rework the old ways, to design creative means in order to show the power of legitimate fieldwork. We need this legitimacy in order to publically demonstrate and understand why a haunting occurs under certain situations. The time is now to seek those cultural "signs" in haunted space. And the time has ended for the demands to "show us a sign of your presence"!

A Pragmatic "Spirit" of Inquiry

As the world turns well into the 2nd decade of the 21st century, there is a new twist to research: serious research about haunting phenomenon, "spirit" manifestations, and "apparitional experience". This is no "ghost hunt"! The designation of meaning is not simply an issue of entertaining correspondence to the real world and its uncanny attributes. There is now a creative process of interaction with than largely unseen world, yet something within the ordinary and beyond the paranormal.

This exploration adopts a pragmatic stance. It focuses on how particular methodologies of inquiry may alter the present meaning of reality:

> **"Knowledge is no longer conceived as something passive, but is more like an action; it affects things" (Baert 2005:163).**

In archaeology, this has involved a more open critique of fieldwork, and the re-consideration of underlying assumptions about the past and what remains. It is this "sign" of a turn of inquiry that I will consider here.

This pragmatic spirit must be grounded in the social sciences if we affirm that a haunting is another form of cultural expression, rather than a change in the physical environment. The use of a pragmatic philosophy in fieldwork at haunted locations means that we must remain open, developing projects that avoid attempts to limit dialogue and outlook, such as a rigid skeptical approach.

Two important concepts in this pragmatic approach include "cue" and "frame". These concepts refer to specific contexts in which interpretation can occur. The manifestation of past "signs" may act as a framing device (a particular haunting context), providing various "cues" as to its significance and meaning.

This refers to what exactly is taking place at that specific moment. This context, this moment in time, this investigative opportunity, implies human social practice that is structured according to space, time, and cultural parameters.

A haunting cannot escape its social ties to the past. Contemporary reality cannot be separated from the social aspects of a research and exploratory inquiry. This research must not be explored within the confines of a "walled" laboratory. It must be based on experiences in the field:

> **"But anomalous experiences, whatever their nature, are inextricably implicated in precisely the social processes and contexts which cannot be reproduced in laboratory conditions" (Wooffitt 2010:73).**

The notion of a "detached" observer, so common in "ghost hunting", through an over-reliance on technology and a "watch and wait" attitude, must be replaced with an emphasis on social interaction, governed by contextual performance practices. We must build our cartographies of spectral space and incorporate them into the reality of the present.

Ghost research can realize its full ethno-archaeological potential as a legitimate form of inquiry by re-configuring its "ghost hunt" mentality. It must re-attach itself, from any paranormal event, to a conscious socially-active science of human inquiry. It must explore these continuing remains of past humanity through a performance in space, and not simply a measurement of that space.

Ghost research, and its sociable focus through archaeology, can help to free us from our complacency to really interact with past presence. We can do this by remembering that social relations in haunted space are not naturally-occurring, or inevitable because of our technology.

The gathering of legitimate data during fieldwork is not a simple "chain of events". A pragmatic philosophy in fieldwork involves a series of parallel, connecting lines of inquiry. These lines of inquiry begin in a particular space at a site. There is an interpretation of that space through various meaningful lines of inter-disciplinary practices.

These inter-disciplinary practices link known and unknown cultural contexts from anthropology (the concept of culture), social geography (landscape phenomenology), theatre (site-specific performance), biology (morphogenetic fields), and archaeology (structured layers of production and occupation). These threads of inquiry are re-woven into a meaningful model of re-producing that particular space in the present.

These investigative practices in particular spaces construct semiotic relations. All communities have regular repeatable patterns and social fields of meaning-making space. These patterns are typical of that particular community, helping to construct and define it, and distinguishing it from others in other spaces at other locations.

But we must acknowledge that much of these patterns and social fields as an "apparitional experience" is politically-laden (controlled by particular groups), economically-impressed (the business of "ghost tourism"), and socially-motivated (peer pressure and prestige). Once we understand this, we can open new options for a place to be defined as haunted by past presence, and why some remain in this contemporary world. This understanding becomes the core of a pragmatic sensitivity to and philosophy of a new approach to haunted space, and its production.

Table of Contents

Photographs

A Warning "Sign"

Many of us who investigate haunted space are aware of the resonances and associations that are connected with particular places by others. This is the popularly-imagined "haunted site". But this popular form of "ghost hunting" must remain separate from those investigations that focus on the production of past space which, I propose, should be the concern of serious ghost research.

A field investigator must distinguish between the production of haunted space and the consumption of that space by ghost tour operators and para-events in these haunted spaces. A serious investigator must deal with the real past, the source and production of space-making, not spatial entertainments that have become popular today.

It is not within the field of serious ghost research to deal with (or be involved in) the popular consumption of the "paranormal", or its commercial use in ghost tourism, para-celebrity events, or popular reality TV shows. These manifestations are pre-conceived notions belonging to the present, and immersed in economics, not research. Such responses to the popularity of the "paranormal" treat the presence of the past as a commodity, a commercial resource for present consumption, purpose, and interest.

Serious ghost research, a concern with the production of haunted space, is meant to be a source of knowledge acquisition. Let's relieve ourselves from this popular, commercial, sentimental, inspiration-seeking, and subjective responses to the past, and its presences. Let's separate them from professional and serious work. This is not a condemnation of that popular "paranormal" attitude. It is a search for relevance in fieldwork.

We must maintain a form of relevance, both for ourselves and for those we study in the field. We must make that form of relevance accessible and acceptable to academia, and to those who follow a "paranormal" stance. To do otherwise, would do a great injustice to those who still remain after the events in their lives have ended, some perhaps long ago.

To think and work in that subjective and entertaining mode has little to do with what (and who) may actually remain of the past in haunted space. Let's just be concerned with the past itself in those spaces considered haunted by lingering presences. I am directing these statements to those who consider ghost research a legitimate and scientific endeavor. I am not trying to change those who hold other views.

In our fieldwork, called "ghost excavations", we treat the presence of the past (including "apparitions") as a natural fact. We consider these presences ethnographic informants. It is they who have produced a particular haunted space. In the field, we participate in their cultural expressions, with their "signs" of communication. We also observe and record their "behaviors" and "practices". We view these manifestations as "signs" of our immersions into their culture as recognizable to them, and the acceptance of our identity. Several contemporary ethnographers have treated "spirits" in this way, as informants during ethnographic fieldwork.

This is a focus on a social (not "paranormal") component. In developing the social realities of the production of haunted space (as I previously did with Gettysburg, see Sabol 2008), we can facilitate the mediation and communication with "who" remains after the events of a particular socially-produced space are ended.

An Alternative Context of a Past Landscape Vision

The production of space is a view of landscape, not as a particular way of seeing, but as a specific means of producing a cultural space: how it is created, negotiated, and (in some cases) contested. Landscapes are created by people, not "otherworld entities". This is an occupation of space through their experience, and their engaging the world around them. It makes little difference the extent of this occupation. It is the experience that counts.

What remains after a particular occupation/production is historical (the narrative), archaeological (the material/sensory remains), and haunted (what still manifests). This is what lies above, below, and between what was, and what is.

My research focus is not on the perceived, a landscape of views and vistas. It is on the landscape as it is negotiated today, through performance practices, with what (and "who") is left from past productions of particular spaces. The experience of this production of space is too important (and interesting) to be confined to a particular time (today), space (as it is observed today), and method (its contemporary measurement).

Any analysis of this past production has to be contextualized: the way people, as cultural beings, understood and engaged within these spaces, dependent upon a specific time in history. What remains after that time in history, are the remains of that time, nothing else!

Landscapes, as various cultural productions of its spaces, are thus polysemic, and include not only artifacts and architecture, but also the structure and processes of social construction and reconstruction. This production of space produces certain "signs" that remain of those various productions. This (the cultural "signs") is what haunts those spaces.

This is an alternative, and not a "para-normal", way of documenting the experiences that remain embedded today in the past productions of the spaces of a landscape that has become haunted by continuing past presence. This alternative, a focus on manifesting past cultural "signs", is a **"technology of memory" (cf. Thomas 1993).**

The production of space becomes a vehicle for a continuing residual and sometimes active re-appearance of remembrance (as "signs" of past cultural memory). This permits the projection of manifestations of these remembrances into the future as, I propose, a situated cultural haunting. This past memory creates social and mental fields of past cultural knowledge.

This "technology of memory", dotting the spaces of a haunted location, is a continuity with past social context. It is not the technology which measures ambient change, such as a deviation from a norm that is never established for a particular space, in or through time. The reader is invited to explore this "technology of memory" as the ways in which people in the past differentially-engaged and empowered space, creating, as a future manifestation, a haunted landscape.

The taking and recording of simple contemporary measurements of a space with electronic devices cannot recognize, through fluctuating readings, the dynamics of a landscape that is formed through various past cultural contexts. As Kuchler (1993) suggests:

> **"when shifting our attention….to the process of remembering, landscape can be seen….as the product of this process which is forever being transformed in accordance with a culturally constructed template" (1993:104).**

The result is a cacophony of voices, experiences, and "signs" of cultural expressions that have produced the landscapes of today, be they haunted or not. This has resulted in the mobilization of different histories in a space. These histories cannot be measured by a detachment to space through the use of scientific instruments. Space must be experienced by performance acts of similar resonance!

Photo 3: **Why has this Contemporary Peaceful Landscape Become Haunted?**

Photo 4: **Is This Culturally-Constructed Template the Reason?**

A Sense of Science

Science is not simply black and white. It is not: you do it a certain way, or use scientific devices, and that is science. Contrary to many "ghost hunters" beliefs, there is no unified scientific epistemology or field methodology! Science is a collection of divergent researchers from different fields who employ a variety of methods to explore a multitude of problems. This is a pragmatic approach.

Science is pragmatism in principle, but many times not in actuality. In some, if not many, cases the practice of science reverts back to black and white. Skepticism is like that, and a skeptical approach to ghost research is basically black and white. To provide documentation in ghost research, black and white science requires one must do it their way, not a way, or it's the highway!

Yet, it has been pointed out, in many cases, that anomalous experiences (including a haunting) **"are inextricably implicated in precisely the social processes and contexts which cannot be reproduced in laboratory conditions" (Wooffitt 2010:73).** It is not a simple case of a white lab coat (and a pristine environment) which illuminates the darkness of haunted space!

It is, I propose, the production of space by cultural beings, both past and present that does it! It is this exercise of daily cultural practices in space that produces much of a future haunted space.

Furthermore, expertise in one discipline does not automatically translate to competence in another. One often hears that there are no experts in ghost research. Why, then, do many "ghost hunters" (probably the vast majority) use electronic devices in the field that are designed for applications in other disciplines? In a "ghost hunt", where is the theory that tests what these devices measure, as a "sign" of a haunting, at a perceived haunted location?

The laws of physics are said to operate in a uniform way across the planet, but cultural systems, the basis of the human production of space, varies. There is no one "uniform" culture, or one common cultural "sign". Anthropology is the science which studies this human variation. And archaeology is the science which unearths what's left of particular cultural productions of space.

Both sciences, one of culture (anthropology), the other of the remains of the past (archaeology), stress the importance of not developing theories, hypotheses, and methodologies of uniformity. Why, then, do "ghost hunters" use electronic devices to establish baselines (and deviations) based on a uniformity of space, and a lack of acknowledgement of cultural diversity in the production of that space?

In a "hunt", there is no theory development, or subsequent test in particular haunted spaces. What is measured in these spaces is a means to achieve uniformity, not test diversity. It certainly does not seek answers to the question of the production of haunted space, nor to the manifestation of its "signs".

A "ghost hunt" is anti-pragmatic, a standard black and white attempt at proclaiming the use of a scientific methodology through the collective application of contemporary technology. There is no "ghost gear"! It has not been proven scientifically to detect a past presence.

I pose a question for these "ghost hunters": why not test for the reasons why a particular past presence might remain in a specific space at a clearly-defined location? This is testing for diversity, not uniformity. It is based on a particular production of space, a production that varies from one space to another, from one culture to another. This type of ghost research is not a baseline that deals with the uniform measurement of haunted space!

One means to do this is through an "extended science" approach (Braud and Anderson 1998). This approaches encompasses a much wider spectrum of analysis, including the fieldworker's own experiences. It is an example of a pragmatic approach.

An extended science approach meets the requirements that philosopher Ken Wilber (1983) describes as valid data acquisition in scientific inquiry. A valid data acquisition incorporates three elements. These include:

- **<u>"Instrumental Injunction"</u>: "This is always of the form, 'If you want to know this, do this'".**
- **<u>"Intuitive Apprehension"</u>:** This is an **"immediate experience of the object domain....addressed by the injunction".**
- **<u>"Communal Confirmation"</u>: "This is a checking of results....with others who have adequately completed the injunctive and apprehensive strands" (Wilbur 1983:40).**

Wilbur defines science as follows: **"by 'science', let us explicitly mean any discipline that conscientiously follows the three strands of data accumulation and verification..." (Ibid: 62).**

In a "ghost excavation", we use all three of Wilbur's strands to document what is left after a particular past production of space:

- We use a "storyboard" design to develop contextual and resonating scenarios that conform to a particular cultural structure and cultural "sign" process in a particular layer of the past production of space.
- We use RT-EVP recorders to obtain an immediate field auditory experience of any "sign" manifestations relative to a particular scenario we just enacted.
- This is recorded and experienced by the team who had participated in that particular scenario, and only accepted as documented if all participating team members had (and recorded) the same experience.

In this way, we document what remains of a past production of space. By documenting the structure and process of investigative performance through the enactment of the "storyboard", we can, in the future, re-iterate these same acts. This further substantiates the data accumulation relation between contemporary performance and past production.

An Archaeology of a Future Haunted Space

The investigation of haunted space is like, I propose, archaeological excavation. Both cannot be modeled on the physical sciences with its broad spectrum of measureable variables. An excavation is limited by what remains in the archaeological record: the remains of discarded material cultural artifacts, and what physically exists in ruin.

Likewise, in a haunted space, what is left after the events of a life are traces of "habit memories". This is a partial record of how a particular space was originally produced through human acts. The full range of social and cultural acts are not available to be documented and analyzed.

The "excavation" of this haunted space is like "striptease". It is the "peeling away" of what lies hidden. It's knowing what is there (what happened there) based on prior knowledge (research). But it is done with an eye for intent and intense interest.

What is left after the event of "stripping away" may surprise. The pleasure comes in seeing more, as less is what always remains from the initial act. What once lie hidden is brought to light, spotlighted as center stage. It is the "excavation" into a specific haunted space, focused on particular individuals. Though the audience (contemporary investigators) is distant from performance (past acts), the experience (and its recording) is close at hand. It is the process of the "striptease" that produces that haunting moment.

Like archaeology, what remains from the past in a haunting is about scarcity: traces and vestiges. Past presence, as the production of past space, leaves (in these remains) a transient, fragmentary life. It is a life that is slowly disappearing, becoming repressed, as new producers of space become dominant.

There is a need to re-construct from the ruin some of what was produced there. These are not "ghosts", as "para-normal" beings. They are human presences. The work of production is a cultural performance. It involved human choices of how to perform, and what to enact, in order to produce certain meanings. It involved a commitment to context and resonance to a particular belief system (a "sign system") to communicate this production.

Ghost research, like archaeology, is based on what has been observed and recorded of the past thus far, the "signs" of presence. That this presence is incomplete is normal, not "para-normal". This fact is to the benefit of both types of fieldwork. It allows an open forum for continued work in the future and, like science, the work is never complete. All the answers are still not known (and probably will never be). That knowledge and insight do change, with the input of new ideas, concepts, and data, is part of the process of constructive inquiry.

Once upon a time, archaeologists unearthed the past through excavation. Today, archaeological field performances can open a space to a future manifestation of the past. This is more than the residual elements of the "ghosts of place". It is an exploration into the continued "afterlife" (not of structures, burials, or artifact assemblages), but of forms of (human) life. It is working with what remains of these forms of human life.

Archaeology and ghost research are capable of observing the patterned residues of the cultural expressions (or "signs") of what is left after the event. But ghost research can observe (and record) some aspects of interactive and past human presence. The thoughts and verbal expressions of people do not end at a particular physical time. This extension of presence was a central concern for anthropologist A. Gell, who writes:

"A person and a person's mind are not confined to particular spatio-temporal coordinates, but consist of a spread of biographical events and memories of events, and a dispersed category of material objects, traces, and leavings, which....during a biographical career....may prolong itself long after biological death" (1998:222).

It is not the "ghost" as such that attracts future attention for archaeology. It is an engagement with past presence itself that allows a manifestation to attain social importance. No longer are we confronting audiences with sites that evoke death. Within the decay of ruin, in the spaces of particular locations, there are these forms of past cultural life, though they are not always present.

They become present – as a potential future – through non-evasive excavating performances. This is, I propose, part of the **"archaeological imagination" (Shanks 2012).** The definition of the "archaeological imagination" is:

"To recreate the world behind the ruin in the land, to reanimate the people behind the sherd of antique pottery....rotted in a sensibility, a pervasive set of attitudes towards traces and remains, towards memory,

time and temporality, the fabric of history" (Shanks 2012:25).

This is not an imaginary recovery of the remains of the past. By participating with the remains of presence, the past is allotted a future. It becomes more than a museum specimen, an object encased in glass. Presence is also more than an interactive exhibit. It is a living testimonial to survival. As participating archaeologists, we become characters in a past story, inhabiting more than an "apparitional experience". It is the immersion of our own lives, during the excavation process, with those of the past.

The fieldwork begins in a liminal position, betwixt past and future. This is a space of alterity, a state of becoming: being in between where things are neither fully present or fully absent. These are traces and vestiges that linger, echoing "signs" from the past. When contextually performed, these "signs" become the actuality of "what" and sometimes "who" remains from earlier times. In this sense, the past, through the present, becomes linked to a particular future identity, and to particular groups of people. This is an archaeology that delineates archaeological material in a manner that deviates from conventional academia, but NOT the excavation results.

As an archaeologist, I want to know what comes immediately after the event of "excavating" performance, using that connecting context to the past to serve as a future baseline for the continued work with the active presence of the past.

This is working with the remains of forms of life that we recovered, leading to a future engagement with them, as the continuing story of the afterlife presence of the past. The performance becomes a means to re-animate the presence of the past for future iterations of knowing what was, and how it was in the past. This is acknowledging its presence, and providing future direction. We must develop a performance repertoire for dealing with particular spaces in ruin (haunted), what remains (residual or interactive), and what practices of retrieval are necessary.

This fieldwork, as "excavating" performances, is a pragmatic approach to the production of space, and what remains as the haunted space of former productions. It is archaeological work. Yorston, et.al (1987:107) articulate four principles for a pragmatic approach in archaeology:

- It should be humanistic.
- It should be context dependent.
- It should make free use of hypotheses.
- It should use theory as a "leading principle".

These four principles can be applied to ghost research. If used, it would change this research, I propose, from a "ghost hunt" (largely for entertainment) to a serious research and field discipline. Ghost research must focus on:

- Apparitions as past interactive cultural presences who were (and continue to be) actively involved in the production of particular spaces. This production (and its manifestation today) is <u>not</u> para-normal phenomena. The traces that remain, I propose, are not caused (in particular instances) by psychological processes (emotional, cognitive, and motivational influences), certain environmental triggers (electromagnetic fields, infrasound) or demonic forces.

- The context of a haunting is based on how a space was produced in the past, as people **"are immeshed in a range of cultural, social, and interpersonal activities" (Wooffitt 2010:73).** A haunting, manifesting today, is based on this past production.

- This hypothesis of socially-produced haunted space, and what remains of that production through the contemporary manifestation of recognizable human "signs", is tested in every "ghost excavation" at haunted locations.

- This is a theory of haunted space that is based on the production of semiotic "signs" in particular spaces, the retention of these "signs" through time, and their manifestations in response to similar (and resonating) "signs" by contemporary investigators.

The particular concern for ghost research must become how these "signs" "ghost hunters" create for a haunting ("orbs", light anomalies, shadow people, EVP transmissions, etc.) compare to the "signs" or meanings that were part of a past reality that resulted in the production of the particular past space that one is investigating.

The crucial questions are these:

- Are these manifesting "signs" a product of what remains from a particular past production? Or,

- Are they manifestations of the technology and beliefs in that technology that are used in the measurement of that perceived haunted space?

By testing within the context of a social structure from a particular past culture (such as the "culture of war" of the American Civil War), rather than a correspondence or adherence to some contemporary empirical reality (the use of measurements to define a particular quality of space) allows us to expand and deepen the nature of what remains.

Of special interest in this archaeological pragmatics applied to the past production of space is the notion of the "sign" as a signal for the contextual existence of a particular presence. This becomes crucial as a means that associates a particular manifestation with a particular social situation and relationship. It is a "sign", anchored in the past, which is brought forward by a contemporary act that resonates with a specific past act.

Thus, "signs" from two temporalities (past and present) function as both representations of a past reality in the present, and as one created in the present that recovers that past reality. The "signs", and their meanings, complement one another.

A contemporary performed resonating "sign" has agency because it re-generates, I propose, those other signs from the past. The control of this process of manifestation, through "excavating" performances via the development of a "storyboard", permits the fixing of meanings to these manifestations of "signs", as part of the remains of what is left from a past production (i.e. a "haunting").

This assignment of meaning to a particular manifestation of a "sign" (as past presence) is not a simple cause-effect relationship. It is a creative act, a craft of interacting with the real structure of social process of a past culture. This fieldwork is not passive as a monitoring or measurement of space, or a watch and wait (a "spectator view") for something to happen. It is action. It is doing something specific that follows what occurred there in that space in the past.

Archaeology occupies a unique position, atop an excavation, looking down sometimes deep into the past. This surface stance is quite paradoxical, whereby something can be there, even though it is not visible (physically-unexposed), until it is unearthed through field performance practices.

This "exposing" the past (as a fragment, trace, or vestige of what was), literally clothing the bones of contention and uncertainty, is not a deep "dig" into the earth, though it is "digging-deep". Today's archaeology, as a site-specific performance in haunted spaces, involves surface probes into the palimpsest of the past. It is the recovery of the "signs" of a presence from the past. What remains of the past production of space is a semiotic landscape: any space with visible inscriptions (or "signs") that are made through deliberate human cultural intervention which provides meaning-making spaces at a location.

Archaeological field practices involve three complementary modalities that can work with this semiotic landscape. These are, according to Jean Molino (1992):

- **"aesthetic dimension"**- This is the engagement of the data in the field in order to reconstruct the underlying past phenomenon.
- **"classification dimension"**- This is the production of symbolic models to explain the phenomenon.
- **"poetic dimension"**- This is how meaning is produced in the production of space. The traces that are recovered are linked to human activities.

According to Molino, **"it is this triple anchorage that links archaeology to the semiology of symbolic forms" (1992:27).**

Is this exposed presence more than a re-constructed time travel? Is it live, alive, and real? Does it become the notion of reality of those, once thought dead, as active actors of past cultural ways? Does "presence" continue to perform today, as if it were still yesterday? Can we read the "signs" of this past presence? How is all of this related to the production of space, and the production of haunted space? Read on and "witness" what may remain in a haunted space.....

"To Be or Not To Be": Is it Real or Fantasy?

In "A Theory of Play and Fantasy", anthropologist Gregory Bateson (1955), argued that a crucial stage in the evolution of communication occurred when **"the organism gradually ceases to respond quite 'automatically' to the mood signs of another and becomes able to recognize the sign as a signal…."(1955:40)**.

Are we receiving "signs" of past cultural expressions at some locations without recognizing them as communication signals? Instead, do we label them as a paranormal event, a ghostly presence, rather than a manifestation in the production of a particular past space that remains active today? Such material remains <u>are</u> part of the archaeological record of what's left of the past at these locations. Call them a haunting, but it is still what survives as expressions of human communication.

As an archaeologist, I am not so much interested in the documentation of these "ghosts of place", as I am in the production of this haunted space, its continuing development. The past is not always dead and buried, and in ruin. At some locations, the production of space continues, as "signs" of life remain.

These "signs" are not complete "portraits" or copies of the past. As Walter Benjamin states in **"Theses on the Philosophy of History:**

> **"To articulate the past historically does not mean to recognize it 'the way it really was'. It means to**

seize hold of a memory as it flashes up at a moment of danger".

That is why much of our work, the "ghost excavation" is conducted on battlefields, especially Civil War battlefields. The battlefield was a **"moment of danger"** for many. We want to document what is left of that "moment of danger" today, through the communication of "signs" that indicate those memories of battle.

Are these "signs" the communication signals of dead individuals? Or, are they merely imprints on the environment caused by some physical (and natural) process? What or "who" produces these "signs" in spaces perceived as "haunted"? Let's "unearth" some possibilities.........

The Record of a Haunting

We must get past the introductions, as we pass-up on the technology. After all, the past continues for whomever happens to be living with the idea of presence. It is about us and past presence, truly not an anomaly or something that we pass-off as "paranormal", something beyond our recognition and understanding. For the "anomaly" is within us all the time, as we recall those days of yesterday as they pass through our memories.

Our contemporary view of "then" and "them" is <u>not</u> new, just our relationship with that presence, replacing another age with an older one. It is just re-thinking about what still remains as memory. The past, then, is not a sequential series of events. It is not about history, as a rational and labored investigation of past acts and events. It is not even a coherent record of this research.

The past is a selection of visions of some trace or vestige of particular yesterdays. This memory is what haunts us. It is also what links us to the manifestations of other memories at haunted locations. Shakespeare's historical works are not histories of men and events, but rather memories of humans whose acts haunted them, as Shakespeare's writings haunt us today. We remember the memory of reading certain fragments of his prose and poetry.

In an investigation of a haunting, we must go beyond the record of recording and measuring the data from electronic devices, the sense of something uncanny, and the memory we register in the aftermath of the field experience. We must document these traces, surely, but this presence must be in the form of an archaeological record.

The concept of an archaeological record in haunted space asserts that there exists a relationship between past situational cultural behaviors and the manifestations that occur in this space. Within this archaeological record, there are two important categories of presence. These include:

- A contemporary, and/or contemporary past, material context consisting of still-living agents. These are largely vestiges (or "residuals") of present acts; and
- A historical context of "dead" past presence, perhaps manifesting as "afterlife conscious minds". This context contains both vestiges ("residuals") and traces ("interactive") of presence. Sometimes, these occur simultaneously.

During "ghost excavations" on the Antietam battlefield (at Burnside Bridge) in Maryland, we have recorded manifestations of both contexts. These can be seen and heard on our website at www.ghostexcavation.com.

It is proposed that these remains, as signs of contemporary and historical past presence, are representations of events, acts, and situations that remain as layers of experience and memory from the production of haunted spaces at Antietam, and the battle for Burnside Bridge.

Photo 5: Fieldwork at Burnside Bridge

It is proposed that this same production of space occurs at many other types of haunted locations. Each of these past productions of space requires a <u>different</u> investigative performance in which to "unearth" what and "who" still remains from the past:

Photo 6: Fieldwork in Centralia, Pennsylvania

<u>Photo 7</u>: **Fieldwork at the Knickerbocker Hotel (Linesville, Pa.)**

The archaeological record of these past productions, as a semiotic system, consists of a direct relation between a knowledge of past "signs" in the form of field performance (as "excavation"), and what materializes as traces of interactive "signs" of past cultural expressions.

What makes these remains archaeological is not their age. We do have a sub-discipline of archaeology that focuses on the archaeology of the contemporary past. They are archaeological, however, because they are "dead", i.e., not part of an <u>active,</u> <u>living</u> context. The distinction between an active "living" and an active "dead" context is that the latter remain static as a presence of a particular past production of space.

The context remains a past presence of "signs" of cultural expressions. The past "culture of war" of the American Civil War, for example, remains (in the present) "signs" of the past "culture of war", even though the quantity and quality of "signs" that may manifest may <u>increase</u> through time. This increase of past "signs" is based, I propose, on the <u>recognition</u> (by a past presence) of contemporary "signs" (performed by investigators) that resonate with those of the past.

A haunting is part of the archaeological record because of its status as a source of "signs" that identifies and defines them as archaeological, as opposed to something else (i.e. "paranormal"). This source is based, not on a subjective experience (a "apparitional experience") alone, but on a manifestation's "representivity" to the cultural expressions of a particular culture from a specific past that can be identified as having occupied (for a time) that haunted space and location.

The archaeological record is a contemporary one, but it is derived from past materialities (or "signs" of presence). The question is this: what survives from the past in a particular space of a specific location? This becomes the contemporary archaeological record, the existence of past presence today.

But this presence is neither a ruin in the romantic sense (a remnant of a completed past), or a classical one (a continuity with the past as an imaginative perception). The contemporary archaeological record is based on the past and contemporary production of space. Its documentation is the unearthing of "signs" of this past and present presence.

The Production of Haunted Space

In a haunting, it is important (albeit vital) to consider the production of space:

> **"any activity developed over (historical) time engenders (produces) a space, and can only attain practical 'reality' or concrete existence within that space" (Lefebvre 1991:115).**

This production of space is based on three elements:

- Spatial practices: This is the production and subsequent manifestation of relations between objects (as a physicality of space: natural/man-made features) and products (cultural behavioral acts relative to those objects).
- Representations in space: This is the knowledge of, and order to, those spatial practices. These are the cultural codes or "signs".
- Representational space: These are the spaces that are "lived" through these spatial practices and representations.

This production of space as a baseline for research and fieldwork not only applies to our object of study (haunted cultural space), but also the ways that our own actions contribute to the representation of space (and its defining "signs") in the future. This creates the palimpsest of haunted space, a series of inscriptions (additions) and erasures/suppressions (subtractions) to the content and type of "signs" that manifest in particular spaces.

Space, including the production of haunted space, is not separate from what it contains. It is formed by social relations and acts. These are ordinary, mundane, and habitual (besides the occasional "eventful"). And they are not beyond the limits of human performance, meaning, or comprehension (re: "paranormal events").

What happened there in that space is what remains in the form of vestige and trace fragments of a particular past presence. These remains include the perception of "apparitional experience". There are no ancient Roman soldiers who remain fighting on American Civil War battlefields!

If the activities in a particular space change, however, then the space (as a production) will change too. This is the concept of a palimpsest. It is the inscription of new layers, and the erasure (or suppression) of older, more historical, layers. The production of space is a "layered" experience, a series of inscriptions and erasures.

A new performance produces a different kind of presence, and a different type of haunting. This becomes a re-temporalization of haunted space, as newer (more contemporary) layers replace older (historical) ones. **All** actions which have occurred in the construction of a space remain in it as part of a spatial horizon of meanings, or as "signs" of previous occupation and cultural presence. This results in a stratigraphy of presence, experience, and cultural "signs" in any given space.

The traces of previous performances remain as resonances of that particular space. All spaces of multiple occupations become "haunted" with traces of past remains, though not all pasts still remain (some are permanently "erased"). A space, therefore is <u>not </u>linear because its production, in varying intensities, is recurring again and again. We have recorded one such trace on the Antietam battlefield in Maryland (at Burnside Bridge). The photo below illustrates this concept of a contemporary haunting. It shows a contemporary "jogger in shorts" on the battlefield. This jogger was not there when this photo was taken at around midnight, during a "ghost excavation" at the site.

<u>Photo 8</u>: The "Jogger" at Burnside Bridge

An awareness of this palimpsest process, and its relation to the production of space, is an archaeological sensitivity to space, and what's left after the "events" of production. As Laurent Olivier (2001) has said:

> **"Archaeological remains are inseparable from our present....More deeply still, we are ourselves producers of archaeological remains....We do little more than add a new archaeological episode to the existence of places and things that have often already known a long series of functions and uses....We add new strata of information...."** **(2001:180).**

Many "ghost hunters" simply do not understand this. Unknowingly, in many cases, their non-contextual acts in haunted space do not disappear at the end of an investigation. They remain after the event of the "hunt" is over. Unfortunately, they may form part of a differently-configured relationship between a haunted space, and the historical hauntings that may have existed in that space in the past.

This creation of a new "haunted profile" means that a new series of "signs" may have been recorded in the space. Future work there may mix "signs" of the contemporary living from the historical dead. This production of a contemporary "live" presence, a "horizon of meaning", may be very perceptually at odds with what occurred there in the past. This creates "ghosts" (the acts and the equipment these "ghost hunters" bring to a particular space). This is not the documentation of an "apparitional experience" of past (dead) presence.

Many "ghost hunters" use historical cues as "triggers". But this is, at best, a re-enactment, an historian's point of view. It communicates history and event as a participatory context of action. Our "ghost excavations" are an ethnographer's point of view. This communicates culture as a participant-observer within which actions are meaningful "signs" in particular past cultural spaces.

Most "ghost hunts" in multi-layered produced spaces are what Alexander (2006) calls forms of **"ethnographic displacement"**. This occurs when a fieldworker is **"more engaged in the analysis of space....than in actually experiencing social space as a sincere cultural participant" (2006:53).** This leads to a <u>different</u> production of space and "sign" development. H. Couclelis (1992) compares the difference in the production process:

> **"The space people experience....differs from the objectively definable, theoretical spaces that fall under rubrics of mathematical, physical, and socioeconomic space" (1992:225).**

That is why experiments under controlled laboratory conditions cannot define how a haunted space is produced. Similarly, the same problem occurs in the field on "ghost hunts", during para-celebrity events, and in "ghost tourism" where a space is probed continuously through electronic devices, creating other forms of "signs" in that space. Most "ghost hunts" and "tourism", probing endlessly the same space, fail to analyze how this production can contribute to a new layer of "live" haunted space! It becomes an "ethnographic displacement" in the production of haunted space.

A haunting is a codified series of symbols (or "signs") that represent the unconscious ("residual") and conscious acts and memories of a cultural life that manifests after physical death. These symbols or "signs" are an afterlife semiotics which can be recognized by investigators, once they understand the structure and process of past production.

The goal of fieldwork in analyzing the production of a haunted space must involve (as one of its principal characteristics) the "translation" of a past semiotic system. One form of translation is the immediate follow-up to a manifesting sensory "sign", following a contextual space-specific investigative performance.

This "immediate follow-up" is an **abduction"**, as used by Eco (1990). It **characterizes the logical procedure a person can adopt when they think they have detected a meaningful pattern in events and act upon that supposition" (1990:59).** The contextual space-specific performance (as a "trigger sign") is used as a hypothesis (in a "ghost excavation") to determine how a particular space is produced and maintained.

The contextual scenario that would follow an immediate field reveal would further test that hypothesis. This process follows Wilbur's requirements for valid data acquisition, previously mentioned. We have recorded subsequent "sign" manifestations as a response to our follow-up. You can read about some of these, in various spatial contexts, on our website at www.ghostexcavation.com.

We have "translated" auditory responses (as "signs") of I.M.P. behaviors of the culture of war on various American

Civil War battlefields. This involved changing an "acousmatic" situation, (Chion 2009:465) in which we heard sounds without seeing their origin or agency, into auditory semiotic inter-relationships between the investigator and interactive past presences. This association was established through the concept of "abduction".

We cannot think of, or imagine, a haunted space as a simple location where "ghosts" have been perceived, or where an "apparitional experience" has been reported. Like social space, a haunted space is not a box for haunting phenomena to take place in. It is activity that is produced through continuing activity that is still human in nature. It retains recognizable "signs" of human cultural life from a particular time in history.

The spaces that are haunted by past presences set powerful constraints upon what (and "who") manifests. There is no ancient Roman centurion giving orders to a company of American Civil War soldiers on a contemporary haunted battlefield! That presence of a Roman centurion on an American Civil War battlefield would be a "para-normal event"!

The production of a particular haunting in space is a fundamentally a spatial practice, and that production is cultural, not measurements. This cultural haunting is a layered infrastructure of "signs" which must be explored in its stratigraphic context, i.e. within its particular socio-cultural and historical context!

Photo 9: Ghost Tourism as a Contemporary "Haunting"

The "Signs" of a Haunted Space

The oft repeated phrase, "Show us a sign of your presence", heard on many "ghost hunts", <u>is,</u> in reality, a part of a ghost excavation semiotic approach. But the "sign" phrase is not a technique of "demand and command", but rather a theory of meaning about the production of haunted space. The key word and concept here is "sign", which is not used as a demand for presence (as "do something"), but as manifesting expressions of cultural behaviors in the past.

This investigative stance is part of archaeology, and has been for a long time:

> **"Archaeological studies all changes in the material world that are due to human action – naturally, in so far as they survive. The archaeological record is constituted of the fossilized results of human behavior, and it is the archaeologist's business to reconstitute that behavior....to recapture the thoughts that behavior expressed" (Childe 1956:1).**

The key words in Childe's remarks, and which we use in a ghost excavation, are the following:

- **"Human action":** It is not supernatural or paranormal.
- **"naturally":** It is something not beyond human capacity.
- **"survive":** What remains after the event, act, or situation.

- **"archaeological record"**: a stratigraphy of past presences.
- **"fossilized"**: cultural expressions that remain the same from past to present, as part of that particular production of space.
- **"reconstitute"**: the ability to "unearth" the past as a social performance in the field.

What remains from the past is part of the production of past space. Archaeologists work with what is left of this (these) pasts. These remains can be thought of as "signs", which represent the cultural expressions of past peoples. It is a form of communication that takes place by means of "signs" through habits of action. The concern of an investigation into the production of space, as a haunted space, is to determine how these "signs" that remain and manifest today compare to the "signs" (as cultural expressions) of a past reality of particular individuals in specific spaces that created this archaeological record. The meaning of these "signs" is not interpreted as it is meant to us today, but what it would have meant (and continues to mean) for a past presence.

This approach is a form of pragmatism. It presupposes communication, and introduces the concept of meaning into empiricist methodology. It requires us today, during an investigation into this haunted space, to use belief systems from different cultural traditions, depending upon who occupied a particular haunted space through time. The meaning of these past "signs" must remain relevant today, as it was in the past, for those past presences who may remain.

In an article titled "Archaeological Pragmatics", Robert Preucel and Alexander Bauer (2001) relate archaeological work to the philosophies of Charles Sanders Peirce. They argue that archaeological interpretation involves a semiotic process through the construction of new "signs": interpretation = "sign" production.

Are audio tracks recorded on American Civil War battlefields, such as our recordings at Burnside Bridge on the Antietam battlefield in Maryland, a "sign" of past continuity with "soldiers" who still remain there after the production of battle in that space had ended? Can we analyze these recordings, and assign a particular "sign" significance to them, as manifestations of I.M.P. behaviors of the American Civil War? Can this be called an archaeological interpretation, rather than a paranormal event?

Peirce's idea of pragmatism, published in an article entitled ***"How to Make our Ideas Clear" (1878)***, has as its basic premise that an idea is only clear if it produces the effect of recognition among a community of interpreters. The "idea" of a "resonating storyboard" (what we use in a "ghost excavation") illustrates, I propose, Peirce's idea of pragmatism. The "storyboard" outlines various contextual scenarios (as "signs") that are meant to "unearth" what still remains of the past production of space at particular haunted locations.

On a Civil War battlefield, the "storyboard" (as the use of a pragmatic approach) is meant to identify us to the "community" of soldiers who may remain on a battlefield. We become, through our contextual and resonating "signs", their "stand-in" officers.

And this is what occurred, I propose, during our roll calls of the 11th Connecticut at Burnside Bridge on the Antietam battlefield in Maryland. Quite unexpected, during this same roll call, we recorded a voice asking me, who was portraying an officer of the 11th Connecticut, "Are You Stedman", the replacement commander of the 11th Connecticut?

In most "ghost hunts", I propose, this question would never have been asked and recorded, especially a "ghost hunt" that emphasizes the use of contemporary tech devices, employs "demand and command", and investigates using contemporary logos on their clothes. These contemporary investigative "signs" do not mix with the past productions of battlefield spaces.

A simple rule to follow to document a past "sign" in a perceived haunted space is this:

- To understand its meaning, one must examine the various contexts it was used in the past production of space.

This past "sign" can only become a meaningful one, however, when it establishes a belief that over time becomes a habit of thought. These habits of thought become established for a Civil War soldier, for example, through drills and reinforcement on the battlefield.

Is our interacting to (with) these recorded "signs" a form of contemporary social production of that battlefield space? Will they became a part of the palimpsest of that battlefield? Will our performances, though contextual and resonating, lead to an inscription (addition) of another layer of haunting presence; or an erasure (deletion) of past historical layers?

Is it extremely important that we use the same "sign", as it was used in the past, to interact with these past presences? A pragmatic approach requires us to expand our reality to accommodate those of past presence. This fieldwork is not a form of imposition (imposing our beliefs as "signs" in the investigation of haunted space). It is a form of accommodation (using their "signs"). In this way, the continued production of haunted space is not compromised.

These questions open the door for further (future) fieldwork at haunted locations from this perspective of an archaeological semiotic and pragmatic approach as to what (and perhaps "who") remains after a particular event in space.

All of these potential "signs" stand for or are a representation of the reality of the past (perhaps multiple pasts) and the present. A haunting is a "sign" of what remains from the past productions of space. An interactive presence is a particular form of "sign" from the past. An "apparitional experience" is the encounter of that interactive "sign" of someone performing a cultural expression from their habit memories.

A haunting, the manifestation of an interactive past presence, and that "apparitional experience" form part of the archaeological semiotic process. These three elements add additional meaning to the definition of contemporary reality of a particular space.

The focus of fieldwork in haunted space must be to ascertain how these "signs" provide meaningful expressions of past cultural behaviors. It must be understood that this meaning is situated both spatially and temporally. The "signs" are context-specific to a particular space, as the production of that space. They are also relative to a particular layer of social interaction in that production of space. That layering and context are what makes them an archaeological record of a haunted space.

In order to achieve a pragmatic approach in the "excavation" of this haunted archaeological record, we must consider science a social phenomenon, and the concept of reality one that **"essentially involves the notion of community without definite limits" (Peirce 1984:239).** This means we must seek relevance for a continuum from past, through the present, and into the future. This relevance must be aimed at particular social groups (and/or individuals). This would involve, I propose, those presences who continue to remain in haunted space.

In the investigation of haunted space, we must identify and document the different kinds of "signs" that past humans used in particular cultural settings and situations in haunted space. Different cultures express and deploy (make manifest) specific "signs", and "sign combinations" toward particular ends. The understanding of this is far more meaningful than simple (and largely unproven) notions of measured space as an expression of haunting behaviors (such as EMF levels, temperature fluctuations, etc.).

According to Braude (2003),

> **"the evidence provides a reasonable basis for believing in personal postmortem survival. It doesn't clearly support the belief that everyone survives death; it more clearly supports the belief**

**that some do. And it doesn't support the belief
that we survive eternally; at best it justifies the
belief that some individuals survive for a limited
time" (2003:306).**

In a "ghost excavation", we attempt to communicate with
those individuals who may survive, who occupy particular
spaces, as cultural beings cognizant of particular "signs" that
they recognize and recall from their life experiences.

Braude (2003) states that the **"survival evidence suggests
not simply the existence of *occurrent* mental states belong
to a deceased individual, but also the persistence of
dispositional states (memories, traits, attitudes, abilities,
etc.)" (2003:294).** These "dispositional states" are, I
propose, the "signs" of particular cultural behaviors that <u>can</u>
be recognized by us today.

These states cannot be duplicated by electronic devices used
by "ghost hunters" to measure ambient changes because
these states (as "signs") are **"inextricably implicated
in….social processes and contexts…." (Wooffitt 2010:73).**
Devices cannot initiate or measure social processes. And
these "signs" of social expressions <u>cannot be</u> measured in a
lab. Why would you set-up a controlled lab setting to
determine the existence of a "ghost" (or "apparition") if a
"ghost" did not occupy that space, that lab setting, lived
there, or experienced life there? It is all about the production
of haunted space for a particular entity or group of past
entities!

The "signs" of a haunting form part of the material culture of
a past (perhaps multiple pasts) in haunted space. These

material (sensory) remains or "ghost culture", I propose, is **"the tangible yield of human conduct" (Glassie 1999:41).** These "signs" of past material culture represent, I propose, the beliefs, thoughts, and behaviors (the "occurrent" mental states) of "afterlife conscious minds" of some who survive physical death. They are the **"fossilized results of human behavior"** mentioned by Childe.

A sound, image (or any cultural expression: a certain smell, for example) is a signifier: it acts as a "sign" of a potential past presence in that particular space. But these "signs" have no necessary meaning in themselves. But they hold potential. This potential comes from these "signs" as signifiers that are located in structures of meaningful sets which differ from each other.

For example, on a Civil War battlefield, sound as a signifier is very important, more important than the visual. The production effects of a battle obscured the landscape. It prevented a clear vision of this landscape. Soldiers relied on particular sounds (commands, "soundmarks", such as bugle calls and drumming, and sounds of artillery and gunfire) for purposeful movement on the battlefield.

Today, to be a signifier or "sign" of a battlefield haunting, recorded sounds there must "lift-up over": they must differ from other contemporary sounds in that battlefield space. They must also be "soundings". These sounds must be tied to a particular historical and cultural context in the production of that space. In the case of a Civil War battlefield, these sounds must convey the structure of I.M.P. behaviors of the "culture of war".

Further, to represent the signifier of an <u>interactive</u> presence, these sounds must manifest in context to similar structures of signifiers, enacted in the present by the investigative team. In a "ghost excavation", these are our storyboards of resonating cultural performance acts.

Nothing can function as a "sign" without referring to another element which is <u>not</u> present. This is the structure, the underlying cultural basis for acting in that particular way with that particular "sign". On a Civil War battlefield, it is the I.M.P. behaviors of the "culture of war" (not visibly present) which controls the manifestations of these "signs" in contemporary haunted space.

During the Civil War, a company of soldiers was a tightly-knit community, a "band of brothers". These companies were organized around particular communities and/or geographical areas. The soldiers knew one another. Their cultural "signs" would be known by all. In drill, this company of soldiers were instructed in the "culture of war", the Inherent Military Probability (I.M.P.) behaviors of this "culture of war". These behavioral or processes formed "signs" of how to act in particular battlefield spaces or K.O.C.O.A. (Key areas, Observation areas, Cover and Conceal areas, Obstacle areas, and Avenues of Approach).

These "signs" of I.M.P. behaviors, the structure of a "culture of war", became patterns of production on a battlefield. During our investigations of Civil War battlefields, we document what remains of these "sign" fields of I.M.P. behaviors.

Objectivity and meaning, then, lie not just in simple presence (a manifestation), as opposed to an absence (or in the case of sound, a silence). A meaningful, objective presence of a "sign" of a haunting is based on affiliation (to a particular cultural context), and association (a resonance to specific past behaviors). These are production structures, tied to a specific space, time, and culture.

For "signs" to have any capacity for meaning, however, they must be repeatable and re-produced in the same context as the prior manifestation, as a further re-production of haunted space, as it was originally (the original production of space). In our "ghost excavations", we always repeat our "storyboards". Something that occurs only once cannot count as a "sign" of a haunting!

A haunting may manifest, I propose, during an investigation as a result of contextual "signs" (as space-specific performances) by the investigator, and the "signs" of intent as a response to that investigative performance. This relationship between contemporary investigative performance and a haunting past presence is semiotic in nature.

This semiotic interplay represents, I propose, the innate capacity for cultural beings to produce and understand cultural "signs". These "signs" can comprise such sensory elements as words, images, sounds, and objects that frame the communicative process between the present and the past. Both elements (past and present) contribute to the production of haunted space.

On a Civil War battlefield, for example, we use words (as "roll-call") and sounds ("bugle calls") as "signs" of the "culture of war". We perform these "signs" in specific battlefield spaces (the "K.O.C.O.A.") in an attempt to initiate communication of "who" remains after the event of battle.

A Civil War battlefield was a soundscape <u>and</u> a "semiosphere" (Hoffmeyer 1998). The battlefield was a structured world of meaning and communication. This involved becoming competent of a set of acoustic, olfactory, and tactile "signs", within a variety of semiotic niches (the "K.O.C.O.A.").

We have documented various "signs" of their communicative semiotics. Particular soldiers have responded to our "roll-calls" in a <u>contextual</u> way (as Civil War soldiers). To hear some of these sound semiotics, please go to our website at: www.ghostexcavation.com.

Semiotics can be used in ghost research to display how apparitions <u>still</u> convey their emotions, life experiences, and cultural behaviors in particular haunted spaces. Semiotics is not a new concept. Issues regarding semiotics have been discussed by scholars since antiquity.

In ghost research, we can use semiotics toward the study of the way "signs", as meaningful manifestations of a haunting, continue to be enacted as social relations in the production of space. Gottdeiner (1995) has called this a **"social semiotics".** It focuses on human (not "paranormal") meaningful "signs" across verbal, visual, and other semiotic modalities.

In social semiotics, context is important. No event, action (as a "sign") has meaning by itself. Meanings become manifest through social practices using similar "signs". This enables a semiotic relation to form, and these practices are typical of particular social communities that define and distinguish particular "signs" as distinctive from other communities.

In haunted space, do we use contemporary "signs" (such as "ghost hunting" logos and "ghost gear") to communicate with what (or "who") is left of those who produced that particular haunted space? Of course, not. But many "ghost hunters" do. Why? Is it "paranormal peer pressure", a lack of creativity, a bow to entertainment, or something else? You tell me!

In haunted space, a grouping of "sign" manifestations can be perceived as forming a "memory community", such as (for example) the "culture of war" of the American Civil War. This becomes a "technology of memory". The context of "signs" would represent an effort to communicate (or enact) I.M.P. (Inherent Military Probability) behaviors, or what these "ghost soldiers" would have done (and experienced) in particular situations on the battlefield. Their original behaviors and experiences contributed to the production of particular battlefield spaces, and what may remain after the event of battle and physical death.

<u>Photo 10</u>: The Production of Battlefield Space

A semiotic communication in this space would involve particular manifestations of "signs" of this I.M.P. behaviors in specific battlefield spaces, and made present, I hypothesize, through contemporary investigative practices that use similar "signs" and resonate with these I.M.P. behaviors.

On an American Civil War battlefield, the principal modality of representation ("sign") would be auditory in nature, since vision would be greatly impaired. These would include such "signs" as answering a "roll-call" and verbal responses to specific bugle soundings and drumming.

These meaningful "signs" of I.M.P. behaviors, as a material habitual competence in the "culture of war", permitted these soldiers (time and again) to accommodate these behaviors toward movement and action on the battlefield, especially when coming to a new landscape not previously seen or known. The Civil War soldier, on the move and in battle, was a continual agent in the production of spaces during the American Civil War. And that is why many different Civil War battlefields are haunted.

A battle is institutionalized combat. There are rules that must be followed. These rules are the I.M.P. behaviors. To act otherwise on a battlefield would result in military defeat. Thus, a battlefield has specific patterns of movement, flow, and behavior. These are the "signs" that we must explore and record on perceived haunted battlefields.

The semiotic "signs" (drill, bugle, drum, roll-call, commands) of living the combat situation would readily translate from one battle to another, and would also be the case, I propose, for those soldiers who remain after physical death. Perhaps these semiotic practices on the battlefield, as "signs" of I.M.P. behaviors that survive today are forms of **"habit memory"**, as developed by Henri Bergson.

In the present, the fieldworker must act with "signs" that allow any remaining past presences to recognize them, in order to recall and re-perform these "habit memories", as manifesting "signs" that acknowledge this recognition. This requires the proper context (a specifically produced space in the past), and resonance (the use of particular past cultural "signs"). This multi-faceted approach is one that shows the continued relevance of the past for the many, rather than the few.

Investigative-designed scenarios, like we use in a "ghost excavation", constitute an assemblage of material agents that help us, I propose, to "unearth" potential presence. This social semiotics provides the framework, scenes, and background profiles (based on extensive research) in which our actions and their responses constitute a production of haunted space. It forms part of the palimpsest of a particular space.

The "show us a sign" of paranormal reality TV and "ghost hunt" field practice can become a theory than enfolds the present back to the past. It deserves some social recognition as one process (of many) in the production of a haunted space.

This re-orientation of ghost research toward an archaeological interpretation of cultural "signs" in haunted space requires this pragmatic sensibility to the way a haunting, a presence, and the experience moves to a more complete vision of reality, one beyond the label "paranormal".

This vision is inspired by the work of Dean Saitta (2003), who identifies three core pragmatist principles that are applicable to ghost research, as the study of the "signs" of the production of space at a haunted location. These principles are:

- An experimentation with theory and method. In our research and "ghost excavations" in haunted spaces, we are always "thinking outside the box".
- Meaning through these experiments must be evaluated against experience. This is: what do we sense and record, to make sense, of these "signs" as it relates to the production of space for a particular layer of past occupation?
- Testing in the context of beliefs from different cultural traditions. We explore multi-layered culturally-occupied spaces. We test various hypotheses in the context of their cultural "signs" for meaning, as it relates to a particular production of space.

<u>Photo 11</u>: Testing hypotheses in the Field

<u>Photo 12:</u> Testing a hypothesis in the Field

We don't experiment or test using some <u>contemporary</u> "sign" of reality, such as logos, particular vocabularies, or equipment that was not in use at the time of the cultural layer we are investigating. Thinking outside the box expands and deepens our explorations into the production of haunted space. Using semiotics, we are committed to understanding the culturally-specific ways in which "sign" production and its manifestations in haunted spaces mediate social past presence.

In this process of exploring the production and manifestations in haunted spaces, we acknowledge our own positionality in this production process. This means not stepping outside of history, but using a contemporary perspective. It means <u>not</u> participating as an "objective" observer, detached from the production of experience.

It is "digging deep", but not becoming entrenched in a particular "formula" of investigating this haunted space. The exploration of the production of haunted space is also knowledge production. This is not a representative (or popular use) process of "ghost hunting". Rather, it is a form of action directed toward the different ways a haunted space is socially produced. Ghost research, as another form of human social science, cannot (must not) escape the social implications of producing additional layers of this haunted space.

Any exploration of space necessitates precautionary measures. Even our non-evasive "ghost excavations", which attempts to be relative and resonate with particular layers of past produced past, can be intrusive, and may lead to a further inscription of a particular haunted space! Because

<u>any</u> performance practice produces production (what's left after the event), potential <u>alternative</u> layers, compared to past social occupations, may occur.

With this precaution in mind, let's consider how semiotics can contribute to social communication in haunted space and how this communication may affect the production of haunted space.

Semiotics: Social Communication in Haunted Space

A semiotic approach is taking a liminal position. It is a mediation between what's left of the past, and our relationship with what remains of past productions. Thinking outside the box, a pragmatic semiotic approach to the production of haunted space means not being a detached re-producer of knowledge: the idea that science, and the scientific method, must essentially re-produce the world in order to understand the meaning of reality.

The focus of exploration, through communicative "signs", of haunted spaces is a move from a field spectator (constantly viewing electronic devices and /or video monitors) to a space-specific performer, working with what is left of the past. This is an approach that is based on the philosophy that the value of field performances should be measured by what is the practical outcome of those performances.

This is part of a new spirit of inquiry that pervades the social sciences. This concerns questions of identity, meaning, agency, and practice. Ghost research, to become part of this spirited approach, cannot be justified as fieldwork (beyond the entertaining aspects) on its own terms. The ethics of a disciplined and professional investigative stance must require that we seek to understand (from diverse cultural and social viewpoints) the multiple meanings of past communications as "signs" of presence. And how these "signs" of communication relate to the past productions of a particular space.

While the meaning of "signs" of communication are multiple and varied, they are not inherently ambiguous within a single, specific context that resonates toward a particular space, time, habitual past act, and "counter-sign" (such as our use of a contextual soundmark on an American Civil War battlefield).

The meaning of "signs" across social and historical contexts at a multi-layered site (such as a ghost-hunting baseline sweep, or a video monitoring of reported haunted spaces) can become contextually meaningless as different "knowers" (teams of casual, independent ghost hunters) may engage, record, and document a "sign" in a different, non-resonating context. Casual ghost hunting, or worse, ghost tourism illustrate the problems inherent in a disassociation between theory and data gathering through a lack of hypothesis-testing in the field. And it adds more layers to an already overly-produced space!

The typical ghost hunting phraseology of "show us a sign of your presence" becomes muddled as "signs" of past identity, meaning, and context are frequently "lost in translation", and/or are improperly codified and interpreted. Communication does not end at manifestation. It begins there!

A haunted space is uniquely suited for semiotic analysis, as communication in particular produced spaces maintain their habitual cultural "signs" and meanings over time as particular contextual productions. Like archaeology, ghost research occupies a special (unique) position for the study of the production of particular spaces. Here, the unfolding of a semiotic chain, within a longer time frame, can be explored and analyzed. This is seen as a layering of communication "signs" that extend across and thru various historical periods and cultural horizons, all of which are part of the production of a haunted space.

Social communication in haunted space is not limited to EVP as linguistic or cognitive messages. It also includes the sharing of cultural experiences, emotions, and the unspoken (the proxemic, non-verbal behavior). Communication must be a creative human process, not a demand that merely entertains. It certainly is not a measurement of ambient data, as a baseline for or against presence (or "sign" of a haunting).

A haunting involves many "signs". These include smells, sounds, touches, sights, movement, flow, and embodied engagements (to name a few). But these must be contextual to particular cultural expressions of a specific past act and/or event in the production of a space. These "signs" constitute, I propose, an ethnography of communication (E.O.C.).

This ethnography of potential past "signs" of cultural life of a haunted space serves as a communicative channel, a socio-cultural context which shapes culturally-specific communicative interactions. This socio-cultural context cannot be duplicated in a lab. A laboratory setting is not a contemporary investigative space where cultural expressions as "signs" have contributed to the production of a particular haunted space. And we do not "invite" the "ghosts" to the lab to participate in our controlled experiment! If they were able to "freely" travel from place to place, and one cultural context to another, then that would be a paranormal event!

The production of haunted space is a common, not unique, process. As DeCerteau states:

> **"There is no place that is not haunted by many different spirits hidden there in silence, spirits one can 'invoke' or not".**

The key word here is "invoke", not "provoke"! One way to "invoke", I propose, is to duplicate past "signs" that were meaningful and became embedded during the production of particular spaces. Communication in haunted space is not an independent and paranormal system of "sign" exchange. Communication here is a mode of social action. It is specifically created by interacting human agents in particular situations of contact.

An apparition becomes manifest, I propose, in and through this interaction of "signs", and the experience of it by both agents that caused it. This re-produces the haunted space. In haunted space, as in other social environments, there is no abstract system of codes ("orbs" or EVP's), or a transmission of bounded meaningful messages or phrases (such as "show us a sign of your presence"). And a haunting communication, I suggest, is not a once and done event!

Communication in haunted space is developed through time and constructive efforts in the transmitting, reading, and interpretation of these "signs". The agents of interaction (the investigator and the interactive presence) are jointly co-constructed in space and situation. This co-construction is the production and re-production of haunted space.

Communication requires a sensitivity to the multisensory and pragmatic aspects of the semiotics of a haunting. This includes a comparative ethnography of human senses that produces a shared experience, and an engagement beyond the purely ephemeral. This inter-communication of "signs" is, at first, at an initial distance. But it narrows through "sign" context and resonance.

Current accounts of EVP transmissions through audio recorders and "ghost boxes" provide, at best, a <u>limited</u> view of social communication in haunted space and, with it, a "paranormal" take on human life and life after death. So much of communication in haunted space, as part of the production of space, goes beyond the perceived "words" in EVP recordings. There are "signs" of this everywhere in haunted space! These become the "signs" that we must continue to explore in future engagements with social communicators in haunted space.

The "Signs" of Presence in Haunted Space

"All reasoning is an interpretation of signs of some kind".

- **Charles Sanders Peirce (1839-1914)**

The documentation of "signs" as elements in the production of haunted space provides a useful means by which we consider how things (as sensory elements) "act" through the signification process. This can be viewed as a succession of capable, conventional, and contextual states of being. In doing so, it can provide a unique (and non-paranormal) way to locate, "unearth", and define a haunted space where agency (specific entities or apparitions) manifest as human cultural responses that are localized in cultural expression and temporality for a particular time and place.

The study of communicative "signs" in haunted space, especially one that has multiple layers of cultural production, is about how structure connects to process in social interactions there. A structure is the social way or means of doing something, as individuals participate in an event. Process is the way these individuals use a particular form of doing while interacting in a particular space. These are the cultural expression of a particular structure.

On a Civil War battlefield, for example, the structure would involve the I.M.P. behaviors of soldiers in battle, or how they would perform in particular spaces during combat. This structure is based on the characteristics of the "culture of war" of the American Civil War Period. The process would be how this structure is expressed in combat on a battlefield. During the American Civil War, much of this process on a battlefield is expressed through particular sounds (or "soundmarks") that would initiate a particular structure to develop in a particular space (a particular performance practice, one that is based on that particular "culture of war").

A battlefield haunting is the structure of the "culture of war" being expressed/manifesting (as process) in a particular way that reflects that structure. The process of this past production potentially becomes the "signs" of a haunting. You cannot have one (structure) without the other (process). What is appropriate in a particular culture (structure) dictates how it is expressed (process), becoming a "sign" that was recognized in the past, and recalled in the present as a haunting.

You cannot mix a present structure (such as an entertaining "ghost hunt" mentality) and get (usually) a past process. You cannot document a past process, I propose, without first establishing a past structure in the present. In a "ghost excavation", we reiterate a particular past structure (what was once produced in the past) in order to contextually document what may remain: the "signs" of a continuing process, a past cultural expression of a past structure (as a "haunting" manifestation).

You cannot observe the structure. You can record the process. We observe the process by participating with a particular structure (culture/time sensitive). This is resonating with a particular past production of space that may be involved in producing a haunted space. We test this hypothesis by performing particular structures in specific spaces at a location that is perceived to be haunted.

If a space is haunted by past presence, then the structure and process already exist. Therefore, by chance, one might perceive or record a particular process because the structure exists as part of the past production of space (re: a "residual"). But any active interaction (a "sign" as process) is irrelevant, without establishing the past structure in the present. This is because no context (performed structure= past process) was established to document it.

Through extensive research prior to fieldwork, we develop **"behavioral repertoires" (cf: Leeds-Hurwitz 1989)** which we use as resonating (and contextual) space-specific performance acts in the field at haunted locations. These "behavioral repertoires" are contemporary structures that align with their past counterparts.

Every "ghost excavation" has a storyboard of these "behavioral repertoires" designed for particular haunted spaces, cultures, and time periods. They are meant to invoke (or "trigger") past communicative "signs" (process). These "signs" manifest, I propose, through the social interaction enacted in these space-specific performances. It is the re-production of past spaces (structure and process).

The processes, as communicative "signs", are active and changeable (especially with an interactive presence), varying in degrees of intensity and variety. But in haunted space, the structure, underlying the process, remains unchanged.

This semiotic interaction is an intensely created act (or acts) meant to expose a particular non-visual past form (structure).

In this way, a past process, if manifesting, can be documented in context. This is production, not measurement of the haunted space.

The social act of semiotic relation, collapsing past and present, requires a commonality of understandings, meaning, and a recognition of identities. It implies common "signs" of communication. It constructs this relationship, mediated by human understanding. This is NOT "paranormal". The aim of ghost research should be the identification of the system of structure and process (the people, and the culture, behind the manifestation) in particular past-produced haunted spaces.

A haunted space can be seen as a continuous process of sign generation, its manifesting presences, and the contemporary documentation of those presences. One of the most substantive implications of this process is that people (both living and dead) are co-joined through semiotic mediation. Both entities are dependent upon their part of the "sign" process.

What becomes important is that these "signs" do not simply convey information from one point to another (through time: present to past/past to present). Without the requisite mediation between contemporary "sign" transmission and past "sign" recognition, there is no firm connection to a semiotic communication.

Through an emphasis on the continuity of "signs" through time, the human element (recognition and recall of memory) remains. Human cultural meaning is conveyed and understood. With semiotic communication, the "paranormal" is <u>not</u> needed. It would also verify the idea that a past presence is <u>still</u> being in the world, in a particular haunted space.

When does a "sign" in a particular haunted space become a form of communication from a past presence? Let's look at a "popular" type of location that is often perceived as being haunted: a battlefield. Many former battlefields are today considered to be haunted by what occurred there in the past: the tremendous loss of life, "instant" death, and many of these soldiers dying young (to name a few).

But does the "culture of war" lead to the production of a haunted battlefield? What really is left after the battle has ended, decades into the future? It is more than historical narratives, more than a contemporary analysis of the battle, more than the monuments that dot the landscape, or more than contemporary re-enacted events for tourism and/or cultural heritage? Do memories, both passive (residual) and interactive survive? Are there "signs" of this presence today? How does a semiotic approach create contemporary meanings from the vestiges and traces that remain?

Let's analyze these questions, by looking at our extensive fieldwork at Burnside Bridge on the Antietam battlefield in Maryland:

- Let's define the cultural expressions of the "culture of war" there upon which a set of communicative "signs" may have been produced, and possibly remain even today, more than 150 years after the battle had ended.

- Let's mark a specific group affiliation, the 11th Connecticut, who began the 1st of many Union assaults toward Burnside Bridge.
- Let's define a particular allegiance to the dominant ideology of the "culture of war", its belief system and behavioral patterns: the I.M.P. behaviors of these Union soldiers, or how they would have acted in a particular situation and in a specific space.
- Let's define a specific battlefield space, used during the American Civil War, as a terrain strategy: the "cover and concealed" area near the 11th Connecticut Monument where their 1st assault originated.
- Let's identify a number of communicative "signs" that would have been used there, and recognized by these men as contextual "soundmarks" (in a preparation for battle): bugle calls to assemble the men, the taking of roll-call, as a preliminary action before ordering the assault toward the bridge.

These defined parameters were used by us in a "ghost excavation" into the production of this space on September 17th, 1862. In our investigation of this space, we wanted to ascertain what remained of this event, 150 years after the battle (and the particular layer of production of this space) had ended.

The manifestation of presence in a particular space (such as a Civil War battlefield) allows us to connect to an individual that embodies a specific cultural history with a specific time and space/place in the past. Ghost research is about much more than "things": "orbs", "EVP", "shadow people". It is about people who occupied and produced a particular space in time. It is, and remains, their imprint in history. It is not so important if this footprint is residual or interactive, or a by-product of a mundane, habitual, or eventful act.

Yet, we rarely make a death, and its subsequent cultural expressions, the focus of ghost research. A haunting occurs in a particular cultural location, amid a specific social web of relationships and obligations. A haunting tells us something of the living person, society, lived experience in the past, and a particular death.

Most ghost hunters do not address specific past attitudes toward death, the management of the transition from life to death, and the concept and effect of bereavement on the appearance of a haunting.

All of these factors, I propose, play a significant role on the structure of continuing presence, and "who" remains after the event of death has occurred. This affects a potential future haunting. One example of this is the significant role, I propose, of the "good death", in "who" remains on American Civil War battlefields.

The structural background (the I.M.P. behaviors of the "culture of war") might be called the "cultural complex" of particular haunted spaces. It is this "cultural complex" which also determines what may remain, and what will manifest. This cultural complex (a system of attitudes, ideas, and beliefs), applied to what haunts a particular space, is that soldiers die in the style of their times.

It is when they don't, I propose, is where they may remain (at least some of them) after the event of battle, the production of a battlefield. This particular way to die is an integral part of the production of haunted space.

Most soldiers who died on a Civil War battlefield did not die in the style of their times. That style of death was the "good death". That is why some of them may remain present on those battlefields. The "good death" meant:

- Dying at home.
- Surrounded by family members.
- Burial in the family plot.
- Proper mourning rituals performed by both women and men.

A battlefield, usually far away from home, was not their "home". Those who died later in field hospitals, lingering for some days or weeks, may have received (or experienced) some semblance of a "good death", perhaps by a family member, friend, comrade, or an understanding nurse. Some death rituals may have been performed: a final verbal farewell, a note to love ones, etc.

And some of those who died on the battlefield, if not immediately, may have been comforted in some way in their final moments. But immediate or instant death did not involve any semblance of the "good death". Some of these men may remain. Like all good soldiers, they are awaiting orders to "go home". That there was a reluctant acceptance of inevitable death by many does not negate the power of the structure of the "good death", as a possible reason for the production of haunted battlefield spaces.

Photo 13: The 11th Connecticut Monument (Contemporary View).

Photo 14: Another Contemporary View of this Space

<u>Photo 15</u>: The 11th Connecticut Monument at Night

In order to analyze any semiotic "signs" that may still exist in this Civil War era produced space, I am using the concepts of Charles S. Peirce (Peircean Semiotics). Specifically, this involves the use of a triadic relation of performances that occur as moments in a graded continuum of functional social semiotics. In using this model, we were particularly interested in how this graduated continuum related to the following:

- The production of haunted space during the battle.
- The opening of a communicative channel based on Civil War era cultural "signs".
- How to document these "signs", as signifying the remains from the past event of a battle that occurred there 150 years ago.

These performances are the variety of "signs" that may occur. Peirce identified 66 potential varieties, three of which have gained wide acceptance. These are the icon, index, and the symbol. It is the manifestations of these "signs" that we attempt to identify and record in haunted space.

These particular "signs" are used to identify social order (the structure and process) in the production of haunted space. They form a baseline for how experience is given order in a past space and time. It is this ordered experience that we attempt to document: what remains today from an event in the past. The documentation of these "signs" involve the use of a pragmatic approach: the study of meaning as it is communicated; and the interpretation of this communication in a particular context, and how that context influences what is communicated.

The characteristics of these three "signs" of communication are the following:

- **Iconic sign:** This is how to respond in a particular situation/interaction.
- **Indexial sign:** This is the context in which the sign is communicated.
- **Symbolic sign:** This is the conventional associations in which this "sign" becomes relative.

According to Peirce's triad of performance relations (or "signs"), a number of auditory tracks we have recorded at Burnside Bridge, at and near the 11th Connecticut Monument, appear to indicate a form of communication with (of) particular past presences. These include the vestiges (residuals) of battle (where their assault occurred), traces of interactive responses (their responses to roll-call) and, on one track, a combination of residual and interactive presence occurring simultaneously. This last simultaneous "sign" occurred along the Rohrbach farm road where the 11th Connecticut were ordered to advance toward the bridge (see Sabol 2012 and 2013 for more details on our "ghost excavations" at Burnside Bridge).

Photo 16: The Rohrbach Farm Road Today

<u>Photo 17:</u> The Location of the Simultaneous "Sign" Occurrence

What follows is an analysis of how these communicative "signs" became meaningful as a "sign" of contextual past presence in the spaces of the 11th Connecticut occupation, and its production of space on September 17, 1862. The question we must ask ourselves is this: how a past "sign" implicates the investigator (and team) into a meaningful interaction? This is how the investigative team becomes active agents of communication that form "chains of signification" (Peirce 1998:409).

Peirce identifies three types of agents. These are:

- **"emotional interpretant":** This is a subjective agent. It is based solely on "feelings" toward the sign. This is a typical "ghost hunting" response.
- **"energetic interpretant":** This is an immediate response to a "sign", as a <u>recognition</u> that the "sign"

is <u>interpretable</u> as a single, situation-specific (and cultural) act.

- **"logical interpretant":** This is a generally agreed upon meaning for the "sign", after sufficient inquiries (future iterations) are made. This links "signs" in a chain of hypothesis-testing.

In our "ghost excavations" in haunted space, we strive NOT to be "emotional interpretants". We use the "storyboard" and its contextual "behavioral repertoire", along with immediate field reveal through the use of RT-EVP recorders, to recognize these "signs" as contextual to a past event (structure and process) and immediately act upon them. Through the documentation of this interaction, we keep (or modify) our existing hypothesis (the space-specific performance acts), and reiterate it at a later date. This further tests the validity of the hypothesis.

This follows our pragmatic approach. This is the notion that a theory or proposition must be judged by its observable and/or recordable practical consequences. This is the manifestation of a particular "sign" relative to a particular "behavioral act" in our "storyboard".

As one example, we will use the structure of a roll-call to assemble the men for the attack. This structure is part of the I.M.P. behaviors of soldiers of the "culture of war". We used specific bugle calls (there were 57 different types that were used during the American Civil War) as a "sign" to assemble the men. These bugle calls were contextual to the period of the American Civil War period.

After the bugle calls to assemble the men, we did a roll call of all those soldiers who were killed during the assault toward the bridge on September 17th. There were 39 names on that list. On the first attempt, we got a response from one soldier (Lewis Dayton). On the 2nd attempt, months later, Dayton responded again. On the 3rd attempt, with a different team of investigators (and several months later), Dayton again responded, as well as Pvt. Alvin Flint. Flint's single response, "Ay" was especially noteworthy. Flint was barely 18 when he was killed, and the tone of his voice reflects a shy, frightened boy.

Photo 18: A Photo of Alvin Flint.

Photo 19: **The Roll Call at the 11th Connecticut Monument**

Photo 20: **Mary Becker Holding the Photo of Flint at the 11ᵗʰ Connecticut Monument.**

You can hear Flint's response on our website at www.ghostexcavation.com.

How does this investigative scenario and Flint's response ("Ay") relate to Peirce's three varieties of "sign" communication? Let's analyze this communicative interaction, occurring, I propose, in both directions (from present to past, and past to present through these "signs") as a semiotic interaction:

- The "Ay" response is an iconic "sign". It is a particular way to respond during a roll-call of the "culture of war" of the American Civil War. The response was not "Present" or "Here", both more general "signs".

- The "Ay" is an indexical "sign". It occurred during roll call seconds after his name was called. It occurred in a cover and concealed space where a roll call would have been conducted. It occurred as a prelude before the order was given to charge the bridge. It occurred at the 11th Connecticut Monument, in a roll call of the 11th Connecticut of those soldiers who were killed during that assault toward the bridge.

- The "Ay" was a symbolic "sign". The response was an acceptance of our identity as soldiers in command, those who would have conducted a roll call. We were symbolic representations of 11th Connecticut power and authority, not "outsiders". Its symbolism was also strengthened by the fact that the roll call by us was recognized by the past presence, I propose, of a soldier from the 11th Connecticut.

The "sign" communication at the 11th Connecticut Monument was further reinforced by another "sign", a question directed toward me as I was doing the roll call. The "sign" was the following verbal response: "Are you Stedman"? At the time, we did not know who Stedman was. He was not one of the soldiers of the 11th Connecticut who was killed during the assault toward Burnside Bridge. We subsequently learned that a Major Stedman, of the 11th Connecticut, took command after Col. Kingsbury, their commander, was killed during that assault. It appears that I was identified as that Major Stedman!

This form of semiotic communication, to be a meaningful "sign" of a particular past presence must, I propose, contain all three varieties of a "sign". It must be iconic, indexical, and symbolic. If a "sign" contains all three, it is an ethnography of communication, a past structure of a particular culture. In this particular case, it is the "culture of war" of the American Civil War. Does an EVP recorded on a "ghost hunt" have similar strong semiotic connections? If not, I propose, it is not a "sign" of a manifesting past presence.

Let's further breakdown the importance of this single "sign", the "Ay":

- The "Ay" as iconic "sign" cannot function as such by itself. It must be contextual to a particular structure (form of past cultural expression). Any response will not be iconic.
- The "Ay" could not function as an indexical "sign" without the roll call, in that particular place (the 11th Connecticut Monument on the Antietam battlefield), and that particular time in history (a battle during the American Civil War).
- The "Ay" could not function as a symbolic "sign", without its association (as an identity of control and power) between the "sign" communicator and a interpretant (the investigator identified as "commanding officer" of the 11th Connecticut).

The present meaning of the "sign" of "Ay" is further identified by how it is defined in relation to itself:

- Its quality, as embodied in the communication (the sound of a "frightened boy").
- Its manifestation as a singular physical event (a response to his name in the roll call).
- It follows the cultural rule ("the culture of war") which governs how the "sign" operates (a contextual response in unison to a contemporary, resonating "sign" that establishes a Civil War roll call in a specific battlefield space).

This sign involves not only language use, but behavioral and cultural rules (the structure) in particular spaces. It follows the past production of a past that has become haunted in the present. We further tested this theory of a relation between the production of space and particular past "signs" with the repetition of this particular role call in other battlefield spaces at Burnside Bridge. We did not record any "signs" relative to a roll call response.

We have documented the manifestation of other "signs" in other areas of the Burnside Bridge battlefield. In each of these spaces, we have followed the production of the process of these signs in relation to what had occurred in the past. I will cite a few more examples of this semiotic relation between the production of space during the Civil War battle, and the manifestation of these "signs" today.

Photo 21: "Excavating" the Past Production of Battlefield Space at Burnside Bridge

One interesting semiotic communication occurred along the Avenue of Approach (the Rohrbach Farm Road), the location of the assault toward the bridge by the 11th Connecticut. Here, we recorded both residual "signs" of battle, and an interactive tactile "sign". Both were contextual to I.M.P. behaviors of the "culture of war", and are "signs" of how the soldiers of the 11th Connecticut would have acted and experienced in this particular production of space.

<u>Photo 22</u>: A Contemporary View of the Rohrbach Farm Road

Let's take a look at the first semiotic "sign" a residual recording of the sounds of men fighting along this road. We recorded this "fighting" twice during our investigation at Burnside Bridge. The first instance occurred when we did an initial peripatetic walk through the battlefield. This occurred in the late afternoon.

A peripatetic walk is important as a preliminary technique before the "ghost excavation" begins. The production of space, and its experience, differs through time. This can affect the meaning of any communicative "signs" that may be documented there during an investigation. Paul C. Adams talks about this:

> **"a place-experience that is familiar in one period may be unfamiliar in the next; what is once known can later become terra incognito through the abandonment of normal or frequent relations with a place" (2001:186).**

What was produced in the production of the Civil War battlefield at Burnside Bridge was later modified with subsequent non-lethal activities, such as tourism and recreational activities. Thus, it was important to get a feel for what remains from these various occupations.

A peripatetic walk is one way to accomplish this. It has been used in archaeological survey, and we use it in our "ghost excavations" at haunted locations which have multiple layers of historical and cultural occupations.

A peripatetic walk gives one a sense of place. It is a way of framing a place, and how it was produced through time. It also may help to **"resuscitate a peripatetic sense of place…" (Adams 2001:187).** Walking through the battlefield allowed us to become involved with that space. It allowed us to sense that place through sight, hearing, touch, and smell.

Ours was a **"light peripatetic"** walk, **"whereby one attunes onself….to be sensitive to something and to harmonize with it" (Ibid: 193).** This provided us with a heightened sensitivity to the environment that is today a heritage site for tourism, and not a battlefield where men fought and died. Our walk did <u>not</u>, at that time, <u>presuppose</u> a haunted battlefield, peopled by fighting men.

<u>Photo 23</u>: The Peripatetic Walk at Burnside Bridge

During the walk along the road, the first manifestation that occurred was tactile. One of the investigators felt (and saw) "someone" (not visible) rotate his canteen of water, turning it upside down and opening it. An audio track was recording at this time (we always have the audio open during our walk to record the contemporary soundscape). When we played back the audio, we have the investigator's reaction to the movement of his canteen, and <u>simultaneously</u> we recorded the sounds of men in battle. You can hear these communicative "signs" on our website at www.ghostexcavation.com.

Photo 24: A Photo of the Walk Moments Before the Incident Occurred.

Subsequently, at night, and after the roll call of the 11th Connecticut, we simulated their "charge" toward the bridge along Rohrbach Farm Road. This "charge" was recorded on video, but the visual was obscured by the darkness of the landscape. However, during the playback, we again heard the sounds of men fighting, shouting, and the sounds of gunfire. On the audio track, we have the <u>simultaneous </u>occurrence of past, present, and future. There are the sounds of battle (past), the sounds of crickets chirping and us moving along the road(present), and the sounds of a plane in the distance approaching toward us overhead (future). It appears that we had recorded the unfolding of time onto itself.

The tactile "sign" during the initial peripatetic walk also incorporates the triadic relations of performance outlined by Peirce:

- **Iconic:** The sounds that were recorded (men shouting/fighting; gunfire) correspond to what occurred in that space during the battle, which was the 11th Connecticut's approach toward the bridge (the objective). It's what they would have experienced in that space.
- **Indexical:** These sounds identify a specific spatio-temporal context of the production of a particular space: the sounds of battle along an avenue of approach toward a military objective. The touching of the water canteen would be a logical act for a man in combat: thirst during a charge along a dirt road with smoke and the smell of sulphur in the air.
- **Symbolic:** The touching of the canteen of one of our investigators was an identification of that investigator as a member of the company of soldiers who were participating in that charge. His contextual presence was a "sign" of his participation, which followed the "signs" of I.M.P. behavior in that particular production of space during that specific historical layer of occupation.

This "sign" performance (present) and recognition (past) become links in a particular semiotic communication that has tested a specific hypothesis about:

- The production of space in a particular layer of historical occupation of a landscape.

- The "signs" of what <u>still</u> remain today of that particular production.
- The usefulness of our contextual performance "signs" to reiterate a past structure and process of "sign" production from a particular layer of history that still remains, in <u>both</u> a residual <u>and</u> interactive mode.
- The recognition of our "sign" production to what occurred in the past production of signs.
- The recall of these "signs" by particular past presences as a form of cultural haunting.

Finally, this semiotic communication, between present/past and past/present is a <u>recognition</u> that the "signs" are <u>interpretable</u> as a single, situation-specific act. It also means, I propose, that the past is not <u>separate</u> from the present. Some of the past production of space, in the form of particular "signs" still remain active today.

We will continue to conduct "ghost excavations" on these Civil War battlefields, in a further exploration of these semiotic communicative links between past and present. The results of these investigations will be posted on our website at www.ghostexcavation.com.

The application of this theory of the past production of space, what remains as "signs" of that production today, and the use of similar "signs" in contemporary investigative practice, is <u>not</u> limited to a Civil War battlefield. We can apply the same theory to the past production of other spaces, and we are doing just that in our exploration of other types of haunted spaces. This research is being documented, several hypotheses are being developed, and new investigative "storyboards" are being designed. The documented results, indicating both presence and absence of past "signs", will be discussed in future publications as we continue to test new models in the field.

Summary

Ghost research, as a form of site/space-specific performance that explores the production of haunted space, acknowledges the symmetry of multiple pasts on the surface of the present. We can more effectively address this production, I propose, by re-configuring our research from a form of "instrumental mechanics" (fostered by the peer pressure of doing this research a certain way), and its entertainment bent as one way to get TV exposure and recognition, to a conscious, morally-focused, and socially-active, science of humanity.

In the production of haunted space, the concept of memory, as the recognition and recall of particular social "signs", becomes a central issue. What is remembered, and why many acts are forgotten (the notion of a haunting "silence") opens us up to a field of multiple possibilities in which to explore what remains of past presence. How might we "fill-in" these silences is a major impetus of fieldwork production.

Photo 25: Fieldwork at a Haunted Location

<u>Photo 26</u>: Fieldwork at a Haunted Location

There is also the important issue of who "owns" or mediates the contemporary use and exploration of socially-produced (in the past) haunted space. Our investigations of haunted space become representations of people's histories, their biographies as humans, <u>not</u> "ghosts"!

How these representations ("orbs", "shadow people", demonic entities, "entertaining performers", or "commodities" for economic gain) are produced today for particular haunted spaces, how their lives are reconstructed, and how they are perceived as communicating, <u>are</u> important issues to <u>them</u>, as <u>human</u> beings. It must also be significant to us as responsible investigators of what is left of their humanity!

A pragmatic approach is a path of exploration; its guiding principle is this: what are the practical consequences of our actions in haunted space? This is a question that I ask myself every time I do or direct a space-specific performance at a haunted location. How do these performances contribute (affect) the production of this space in the future? How do our performances affect the individual, the real life behind the image of a "ghost"?

All forms of "excavation" are destructive as well as constructive. A "ghost excavation" is meant to be as least intrusive as possible to what (little) remains of multiple pasts in haunted space. A space-specific performance is meant to resonate with what occurred (or may have occurred) in the past. It "entertains" the notion that contemporary acts do produce inscriptions (the addition of layers) or erasure (the deletion or suppression of a past layer) in the palimpsest that has become a haunted space.

The true value of our work in a "ghost excavation" at a haunted location (or specifically in a haunted space) is measured (not by electronic instruments, or asking for a "trick" to be performed), but through the particular vision of our continuing experience as a cultural human. This vision is squarely centered (as a baseline) on critical experimentation in these haunted spaces.

These haunted spaces are not "laboratories" controlled for the prevention of "outside" influences. They are spaces where the haunting occurred: the past socially-produced spaces! Our work does not end with the experience of experimentation. As James (1995:7) states, this work must appear as

> **"less of a solution....than as a programme for more work, and more particularly as an indication of the ways in which existing realities may be changed. Theories become instruments, not answers to enigmas, in which we can rest".**

It was with this philosophical orientation that I wrote this book. A "ghost excavation", as a form of space-specific performance, working with what is left of the past in haunted space, is meant to continue that pragmatic tradition of relevance, optimism, and experimentation far into the future to extract what remains of presence far into the past.

To understand the meaning of a socially-produced haunted space is to use theory in the study of praxis: defined as situated knowledge. It is using what we know in order to do something. We know the "culture of war" of the American Civil War, its I.M.P. behaviors, the importance of soundmarks on an obscured battlefield, and how these structures plays into the past production of that battlefield space.

What we don't know is how or why an interactive entity manifests there. The measurement of contemporary space does not resolve this issue. Understanding spatial production, what may remain as "signs" of that production, might. This understanding of past production serves as our baseline (what we do know). It builds a storyboard for the contemporary performance of various elements in that reiteration of a past production of particular spaces.

The emphasis on "signs" is a turn away from "images", or an emphasis on the visual, "looking" at meters, photos, or monitors in haunted space. It is a more comprehensive aspect of an "excavation". A "sign" is not always the visual representation of the past.

Such a concept is well-suited for the production of haunted space, where the manifestation of past presence (as a particular identifiable and visible "dead" human) is relatively rare. "Showing us a 'sign'", as part of a produced haunted space, and in the context of a contemporary production of similar semiotic "signs", is a good baseline to further explore other indexes and symbolisms (as cultural expressions) of a haunted space.

As Jack Hunter states, in *"The Anthropology of the Weird"* (**Darklore Vol. 6: 243-253.**):

> **"These types of experiences can be had by anyone so long as they participate in the relevant cultures and ritual situations….It requires our participation in the moment….in order to be experienced"** (p. 253).

Time and again in our fieldwork at haunted locations, it is the significant role of culture, its diversified array of expressions, and our participation in those expressed cultural behaviors and memories (as a production of a particular space), that has allowed us to document and record these past cultural remains. It is these "signs" that we call a "cultural haunting" of past presence. And these cultural hauntings also include those who "haunt" us with their presence from the contemporary past, such as that "jogger" that we photographed on the Antietam battlefield at Burnside Bridge. The question of that "jogger" is this: Is he still alive, or is he the residual image of a now deceased person?

For the moment, that question will remain unanswered. It is a question that we will ask ourselves the next time we do a "ghost excavation" there.........

<u>Photo 27:</u> The Reiteration of a Contemporary Haunting

Bibliography

Adams, Paul C. (2001). *"Peripatetic Imagery and Peripatetic Sense of Place"* in *Textures of Place: Exploring Humanistic Geographies*. Paul C. Adams, Steven Hoelscher, and Karen Till (Eds.). Minneapolis: University of Minnesota Press. pp. 186-206.

Alexander, Bryant K. (2006). *"Telling Twisted Tales: Owning Place, Owning Culture in Ethnographic Research"*. In *Opening Acts: Performance In/As Communication and Cultural Studies*. Judith Hamera (Ed.) Thousand Oaks, California: Sage. pp. 49-74.

Baert, Patrick (2005). *Philosophy of the Social Sciences: Towards Pragmatism*. Cambridge, UK: Polity Press.

Bateson, Gregory (1955). *"A Theory of Play and Fantasy: A Report on Theoretical Aspects of the Project for the Study of the Role of Paradoxes of Abstraction in Communication"*. In *Approaches to the Study of Human Personality*. American Psychiatric Association. pp. 39-51.

Braude, Stephen (2003). *Immortal Remains: The Evidence for Life After Death*. New York: Rowman and Littlefield.

Braude, S. & Anderson, R. (1998). *Transpersonal Research Methods for the Social Sciences: Honoring Human Experiences*. London: Sage.

Childe, V.G. (1956). *Piecing Together the Past: The Interpretation of Archaeological Data*. New York: Fredrick A. Praeger.

Chion, Michel (2009). *Audio-Vision: Sound on Screen.* New York: Columbia University Press.

Couclelis, H. (1992). *"Location, Place, Region, and Space".* In R.F. Abler, M. Marcus, and J. M. Olson (Eds.). *Geographies Inner Worlds: Pervasive Themes in Contemporary American Geography.* New Brunswick, New Jersey: Rutgers University Press. pp. 215-233.

Eco, U. (1990). *The Limits of Interpretation.* Bloomington: Indiana University Press.

Gell, A. (1998). *Art and Agency: An Anthropological Theory.* Oxford: Oxford University Press.

Glassie, H. (1999). *Material Culture.* Bloomington: Indiana University Press.

Gottdeiner, M. (1995). *PostModern Semiotics: Material Culture and the Forms of PostModern Life.* Oxford: Blackwell.

Hoffmeyer, J. (1998). *"Biosemantics"* in *Encyclopedia of Semiotics.* Paul Bouissac (Editor). Oxford: Oxford University Press. pp. 82-85.

James, William (1975). *Pragmatism: A New Name for Some Old Ways of Thinking.* In *The Works of William James, Vol. 2.* F.H. Burkhardt, F. Bowers, and I.K. Skrupskelis (Eds.). Cambridge University Press.

Kuchler, Susanne (1993). *"Landscape as Memory: The Mapping of Process and its Representation in a Melanesian Society",* in *Landscape Politics and Perspectives.* Barbara Bender (Ed.). Oxford: Berg. pp. 85-106.

Lefebvre, Henri (1991). *The Production of Space*. Oxford: Basil Blackwell.

Leeds-Hurwitz, Wendy (1989). *Communication in Everyday Life: A Social Interpretation*. Praeger.

Marsden, Simon (1994). *The Journal of a Ghosthunter*. London: Little, Brown and Co.

Molino, Jean (1992). *"Archaeology and Symbolic Systems"* in *Representation in Archaeology*. J.C. Gardin and C.S. Peebles (Eds.). Bloomington: Indiana University Press. pp. 15-29.

Olivier, Laurent (2001). *"The Archaeology of the Contemporary Past"* in V. Buchli and G. Lucas (Eds.) *Archaeology of the Contemporary Past*. New York: Routledge. pp. 175-188.

Peirce, Charles S. (1984). *Writings of Charles S. Peirce: A Chronology, Volume 2 1867-71*. Bloomington: Indiana University Press.

(1998). *The Essential Peirce: Selected Philosophical Writings, Volume 2. 1983-1913*. Bloomington: Indiana University Press.

Preucel, Robert and Alexander Bauer (2001). *"Archaeological Pragmatics"* Norwegian Archaeological Review. 34: 85-96.

Sabol, John G. Jr. (2008). *The Politics of Presence*. Bloomington, Indiana: AuthorHouse.

(2012). *Digging Up Ghosts: The Archaeology of the Interactive Past.* Brunswick, Maryland: Ghost Excavation Books, Inc.

(2013). *Burnside Bridge: The Excavation of a Civil War Soundscape.* Brunswick, Maryland: Ghost Excavation Books, Inc.

Saitta, Dean (2003). *Archaeology and the Problems of Men.* In *Essential Tensions in Archaeological Method and Theory.* T.L. VanPool and C.S. VanPool (Eds). Salt Lake City: University of Utah Press. pp. 11-16.

Shanks, Michael (2012). *The Archaeological Imagination.* Walnut Creek, California: Left Coast Press.

Thomas, Julian (1993). *"The Politics of Vision and the Archaeologies of Landscape"* in *Landscape Politics and Perspectives.* Barbara Bender (Ed.). Oxford: Berg. pp. 19-48.

Wilber, Ken (1983). *Eye To Eye: The Quest for the New Paradigm.* Boston: Shambhala.

Wooffitt, Robin (2010). *"Towards a Sociological Parapsychology"* in *Anomalous Experiences: Essays from Parapsychology and Psychological Perspectives.* Matthew D. Smith (Ed.). Jefferson, North Carolina: McFarland. Pp. 72-91.

Yorston, Ron M. (1987). *"Theory and Method: Some Observations From a Scientist"* in *Pragmatic Archaeology: Theory in Crisis?* Christopher F. Gaffney and Vincent L. Gaffney (Eds.) Oxford. Pp. 17-26.

Author Biography

John Sabol is an archaeologist, cultural anthropologist, actor, and author. As an archaeologist, he has unearthed past material remains in excavations and site surveys in England, Mexico, and at various sites in the United States (including Eastern South Dakota, the Tennessee River Valleys, and in Pennsylvania). His anthropological fieldwork includes the studies of "spirits" in the religious beliefs of the afterlife among various cultural groups in Mexico (Mixtec, Zapotec, Lacandon, Nahuatl, and Otomi). His acting career includes "ghosting" performances of various characters and scenarios in more than 35 movies, TV shows, and documentaries. He has appeared in the A&E TV series, Paranormal State as an investigative consultant.

He has written eighteen books. These include: *Ghost Excavator (2007), Ghost Culture (2007), Gettysburg Unearthed (2007), Battlefield Hauntscape (2008), The Anthracite Coal Region: The Archaeology of its Haunting Presence (2008), The Politics of Presence: Haunting Performances on the Gettysburg Battlefield (2008), Bodies of Substance, Fragments of Memories: An Archaeological Sensitivity to Ghostly Presence (2009), Phantom Gettysburg (2009), Digging Deep: An Archaeologist Unearths a Haunted Life (2009), The Re-Hauntings of Gettysburg (2010), Digging Up Ghosts (2011), The Haunted Theatre (2011), Haunting Archaeologies (2012), Beyond the Paranormal: Unearthing An Extended "Normal" at Haunted Locations (2013), Burnside Bridge Hauntscape: The Excavation of a Civil War Soundscape (2013), The Gettysburg Battlefield Experience (2013)*, *The Absence Above, The Presence Below (2013)*.

His recent speaking engagements include the T.A.G. (Theoretical Archaeology Group) Conference at the University of California, Berkeley, at the Space and Place Conference in Prague, Czech Republic, the TAG Conference at the University in Buffalo, New York, Exploring the Extraordinary Conference in York, England, the C.H.A.T. archaeological conference also in York, and the GHost Conference at the University of London, London, England.

His investigative reports have been published in such diverse venues as Haunted Times Magazine, Tennessee Anthropologist, and the online journal, ParaAnthropology. He has been a frequent guest on numerous radio and internet talk shows, among them, Beyond the Edge Radio, The Paranormal View, Para X Radio, Blog Talk Radio, The Grand Dark Conspiracy, and Rusty O'Nhiall's "Mysterious and Unexplained" on PsiFM (Australia). He was a university professor in Mexico for 11 years, teaching both undergraduate and graduate courses on the anthropology of tourism. He has also been featured on public educational TV for U.S. and foreign markets, and has worked on international educational documentaries (in Spain).

He has a M.A. in Anthropology/Archaeology (University of Tennessee), and a B.A. in Sociology/Anthropology (Bloomsburg University). He has also attended Penn State University, the University of Pittsburgh, the University of the Americas (Cholula, Puebla, Mexico), and has studied theatre and method acting in Mexico City.

He can be reached via email at cuicospirit@hotmail.com. His website is: **www.ghostexcavation.com** and he can be found on Facebook ("Ghost Excavations with John Sabol").